HOLIDAY HOOPLA
Plays, Parades, Parties

PLAYS, GAMES, FAVORS, PROPS, DECORATIONS, CRAFTS, COSTUMES, AND SNACKS
by Kathy Darling, illustrated by Marilynn G. Barr

With special thanks to Cindy Ricca
and Ricca Family Day Care

Publisher: Roberta Suid
Editor: Carol Whiteley
Production: Susan Pinkerton

monday morning

Monday Morning is a registered trademark of
Monday Morning Books, Inc.

ISBN 1-878279-13-0

For information about our audio products, write us at:
Newbridge Book Clubs, 3000 Cindel Drive, Delran, NJ 08370

Printed in the United States of America
9 8 7 6 5 4 3 2 1

Contents

Introduction

Celebrating the holidays gives us a chance to come together in joy for fun and relaxation. The rituals and traditions of our celebrations lend continuity to our year and highlight the passage of time. In *Holiday Hoopla: Plays, Parades, Parties* you will find a variety of ways to celebrate the special days of the year.

Party plans offer a complete morning or afternoon of fun starting with party wear and decorations that the children can make themselves. You will also find snack recipes that children can enjoy making with your help, party favors, and special games.

Recognizing the star potential in children everywhere, we provide how-to's for holiday parades, including dress-up and prop ideas to create a festival air. You will also find two plays and a mini-play. The plays have been specially created and tested to offer a brief, successful dramatic experience. Children speak few or no lines at all, and are conveniently led in action through the narrator's cues. Easy and inexpensive costume and prop ideas are included.

Taking part in these plays may be your preschoolers' first experience with drama. It helps to read the play to the children first, in story form, so that they become familiar with characters and setting. You may wish to use a highlighter to mark the text for the narrator and the cues for the actors, and you'll want to be sure to have a backstage helper. Preschoolers have very particular ideas about what they are comfortable wearing or carrying so be flexible when it comes to costumes and props.

Don't be afraid to let the children adapt the play to their needs. And don't expect perfection. Remember, it is often the gaffes and improvisational antics of your little actors and actresses that make performances especially endearing and certainly memorable!

All the plays, parades, and parties in this book have been tested and enjoyed by children just like yours. We guarantee these festive gatherings will offer a fine cultural experience as well as great social success! Celebrate!

Halloween Parade

Materials: Dresses, overcoats, capes or large pieces of colorful fabric that can be draped or tied around the shoulders, hats, shoes, colorful accessories such as scarves, netting, boas, gloves, necklaces, earrings, bracelets, old watches, canes, umbrellas, etc.

Preparation: Encourage the children to come to the parade already in costume or set up a dressing room with the materials you have on hand and let the children create their own. Some ideas: Superheroes can tie on a colorful cape and wear a headband. Cats can wear all black, pin on a long fabric tail, paint on whiskers, and clip paper ears into their hair. Clowns need only colorful clothes, a red painted nose, and an oversized hat with bright yarn hanging out underneath. Ghouls can wear a sheet or fabric drape that has a neck hole cut out of the center, then pin on some rubbery plastic Halloween critters. They can paint on fierce faces, mess up their hair and stick leaves and branches in it, and carry along a simple noisemaker.

Halloween paraders can also carry along Flappy Bats (see Party Favors), paper towel tube batons with long orange and black streamers taped to them, or flashlights that have been covered with colored cellophane for parading at night. Parade marchers may also want to bring along all kinds of noisemakers. Check your local library for a selection of ghostly music to accompany the marchers.

Parade Dance

Materials: A large curtain-sized piece of black fabric
(lining material is lightweight and inexpensive)
or an old sheet that has been randomly spray-
painted with Halloween colors, ghostly music

Preparation: Rig up the curtain. Make a slit halfway up the
center, tall enough for little ones to walk
through.

Activity: First have all the children parade through the
curtain, moving to ghostly music or
accompanied by their own scary howling. Then
have them form a circle and chant:
Bright, bright Halloween night (walk in a
 circle, holding hands),
Shake, shake your body tonight (drop hands,
 shake)!
Bright, bright Halloween night (walk in circle),
Stomp away all fright tonight (stomp loudly)!
Bright, bright Halloween night (walk to center),
Scream in delight tonight (raise arms, scream)!

Take It from the Top Party Wear

Materials: Hats, hats, and more hats! Make a trip to your local Goodwill or Salvation Army shop and encourage parents to plow through closets and cupboards for old cowboy hats, racing caps, ski hats, top hats, Derbies, "pill-box" hats, felt hats, sunbonnets, visors, helmets, hard hats, even shower caps and paper party hats. Ask your local fire department, hospital, construction firm, or food service company to donate some of their headgear for the event.

Preparation: Set aside time for a simple yet fun Halloween Day party where the children wear a hat as their party costume. The children will want to try on several hats before they decide which one to wear, so make all the hats available and supply several hand mirrors and, if possible, a full-length mirror.

Activity: Once the children have on their hats, give them a chance to act out their roles. A child with a cowboy hat can gallop on a horse; a ski hat wearer can swoosh down a snowy slope; a child with a feathered bonnet can pretend to be a model walking down a fashion runway; a child wearing a hard hat can pound nails.

Spider Web Decorations

Materials: Lots and lots of string, unbonded polyester batting, plastic spiders and flies (optional), scissors

Preparation: Cut the string into several very long lengths.

Activity: Let the children have fun decorating the room in a tangled mess of spider webs. Show them how to wrap one end of a length of string around a doorknob or drawer pull and then weave it in and out of several pieces of furniture until it is impossibly tangled. Several of the children can stretch and pull apart the batting and drape it eerily over chairs and across windows. Let the children attach spooky spiders and flies to the webs if desired.

Flappy Bat Party Favors

Materials: Toilet paper tubes, Styrofoam or paper cups (just large enough for a tube to fit inside; optional), black construction paper, marker, scissors, treat mix made of nuts, raisins, chocolate morsels or small candies, or the like (optional)

Preparation: Outline two bat wing shapes for each child on black paper, using the illustration as a guide. Make a small slit on either side of one end of each tube and distribute a tube and two wing outlines to each child.

Activity: Have the children cut out the bat wing shapes. Show them how to carefully slip each wing into a slit in the tube. Then show the children how to wiggle the end of the tube to make the bat's wings flap. Put each child's name on his or her bat. If desired, take the bats and tell the children they will be returned to them in the form of a surprise at the party table. Out of sight, set each bat in a cup, then carefully fill the tube about halfway up with the treat mix. Put one flappy bat in a cup at each place setting. Let the children lift off the bat tubes to discover the treats in the cup.

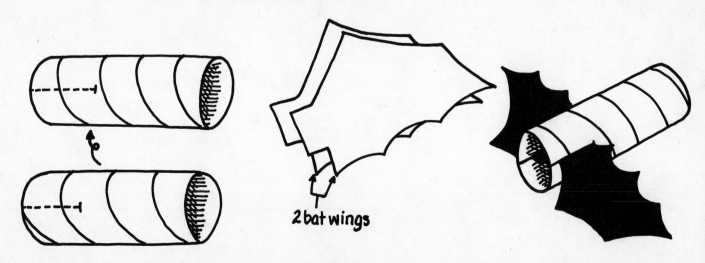

2 bat wings

Baked Apple Ring Snacks

Materials: Baking apples, brown sugar, cinnamon, spoons, forks, baking sheets, knife, peeler

Preparation: Peel and core the apples. Slice into thick rings and set on baking sheets.

Activity: Allow each child to spoon 1 teaspoon of brown sugar onto an apple ring, then sprinkle on a little cinnamon. Bake the rings in a 350 degree oven until the sugar melts and the rings soften. Cool slightly and serve with forks.

Pumpkin Seeds

Materials: Carved-out pumpkin, pumpkin seeds

Preparation: Set out the pumpkin and give each child a small handful of seeds.

Activity: Let each child stand a short distance from the pumpkin and try to toss the seeds, one by one, into the jack-o'-lantern. Toast some seeds for snacking.

Hop the Pumpkins Game

Materials: Various sizes of pumpkins, old tires, boards, Hula-Hoop, rubber ball

Preparation: Create a fun obstacle course by placing the pumpkins, tires, and boards at various intervals. You might also want to hang a Hula-Hoop from a tree limb.

Activity: Allow each child to maneuver through the obstacle course. Have the children jump over the pumpkins, hop in and out of the tires, walk over the boards, and take aim and throw the rubber ball through the Hula-Hoop.

Scarecrow and the Sleepy Pumpkin Patch Play

Narrator: Leaves are turning yellow, brown, and red. Pumpkins and squash are growing big and round. Off in a field somewhere three pumpkins are sleeping. Here comes Scarecrow to try and wake them up.

(Pumpkins are sitting lazily in their patch at center stage with eyes closed. Scarecrow rushes onto the stage waving his arms and shouting.)

Scarecrow: Wake up, pumpkins, wake up!

Narrator: The pumpkins sit up and sing.

Pumpkins: (To the tune of "It Ain't Gonna Rain No More")
I ain't gonna grow no more, no more.
I ain't gonna grow no more.
Harvest time is here I know,
So I ain't gonna grow no more.

Narrator: But Scarecrow says they must grow.

Scarecrow: (Waving his arms wildly) Grow! Grow!

Narrator: But the pumpkins go back to sleep.

(Pumpkins close their eyes again, Scarecrow shrugs and exits. Granny enters and circles the pumpkin patch.)

Narrator: Later that day, Granny visits the pumpkin patch. She is looking for a big pumpkin for her harvest table.

Granny: I need the biggest pumpkin!

(Granny exits.)

14

Narrator: The pumpkins hear Granny and start to grow as big as they can. They all want to be on the harvest table! Later in the evening, Granny returns for the biggest pumpkin. The rest of the pumpkins go back to sleep.

(Granny re-enters and leaves with one of the pumpkins.)

Narrator: In the morning, Scarecrow tries to wake the pumpkins up again.

(Scarecrow rushes onto the stage jumping, waving his arms, and shouting.)

Scarecrow: Wake up, pumpkins, wake up!

Narrator: The pumpkins sing.

Pumpkins: I ain't gonna grow no more, no more.
I ain't gonna grow no more.
Harvest time is here I know,
So I ain't gonna grow no more.

Narrator: But Scarecrow says they must grow.

Scarecrow: (Waving his arms wildly) Grow! Grow!

Narrator: But the pumpkins are sad they were not chosen to be on the harvest table so they go back to sleep.

(Pumpkins close their eyes again, Scarecrow shrugs and exits. The little boy enters and circles the pumpkin patch.)

Narrator: Later that day a friendly little boy visits the pumpkin patch. He is looking for a big pumpkin to make a pie.

Little Boy: I need the biggest pumpkin!

(The little boy exits.)

Narrator: The pumpkins hear the little boy and try to grow as big as they can. They both want to be a pumpkin pie! That evening the little boy returns and takes the biggest pumpkin. And the last pumpkin goes back to sleep.

(The little boy re-enters and leaves with one of the pumpkins.)

Narrator: In the morning, Scarecrow tries to wake the pumpkin up.

(Scarecrow rushes onto the stage jumping, waving his arms, and shouting.)

Scarecrow: Wake up, pumpkin, wake up!

Narrator: The pumpkin sings.

Pumpkin: I ain't gonna grow no more, no more.
I ain't gonna grow no more.
Harvest time is here I know,
So I ain't gonna grow no more.

Narrator: But Scarecrow says the pumpkin must grow.

Scarecrow: (Waving his arms wildly) Grow! Grow!

Narrator: But the pumpkin is sad he was not chosen to be a pie, so he goes back to sleep.

(Pumpkin closes eyes again, Scarecrow shrugs and exits. The farmer enters and circles the pumpkin patch.)

Narrator: Later that day a friendly farmer visits the pumpkin patch. He wants a big pumpkin for the Harvest Fair.

Farmer: I need the biggest pumpkin!

(The farmer exits.)

Narrator: The pumpkin hears the farmer and tries to grow as big as he can. He wants to go to the fair! That evening the farmer comes back for the biggest pumpkin in the patch.

(The farmer re-enters and leaves with the last pumpkin.)

Narrator: And now there are no more pumpkins left! The next morning Scarecrow comes to the pumpkin patch.

(Scarecrow rushes onto the stage jumping, waving his arms, and shouting.)

Scarecrow: Wake up! Wake up!

Narrator: But where are the pumpkins?

Scarecrow: Where are all the pumpkins?

Narrator: All the pumpkins are gone. They are on the harvest table, baked into a pie, and at the Harvest Fair! Scarecrow has no one to wake up anymore. So. . . . he goes to sleep!

(Scarecrow curls up in the pumpkin patch and falls asleep.)

Stage Set-Up

The stage can be defined by a simple curtain. You may want to enlist a parent or aide to open and close the curtain at the beginning and end of the play.

Decorate the stage with fall foliage. Scatter leaves, twigs, and various types of squash and gourds about the stage. To define the pumpkin patch, place a few pumpkins in a circle at center stage. Have the children who play pumpkins sit here. If you want to have more than three children play pumpkins, change the lines so that the granny and the little boy take more than one pumpkin with them when they exit the stage. Always leave one lone pumpkin for the farmer to take.

Characters

Narrator (adult)	Granny
Pumpkins (at least 3)	Little Boy
Scarecrow	Farmer

Costumes

Pumpkin costumes can be made from pillow cases or paper bags painted orange, or from draped orange material. If you use pillow cases or bags, make armholes and then cut up the back so the costumes can be slipped on and then pinned or left open in the back. If you want to, belt a small pillow around the children's middle under the costume for added puffiness. Headpieces can be made by stapling one end of a length of elastic to each side of a paper plate, then covering the plate with green paper leaves.

Scarecrow can wear patched jeans or overalls, a bright shirt, mismatched shoes, and an old straw hat. Stuff plenty of straw into shoes, shirt neck, and pockets and let it hang out all over. Granny can wear a dress and colorful apron, a small sunbonnet, and some granny glasses. The little boy can wear everyday clothing. The farmer can wear dungarees or overalls, a plaid shirt, boots, and a cowboy or baseball hat. A trowel or other gardening tool could stick out of his back pocket.

Props

No special props are needed, but you may want to let the
children make paper decorations such as colorful paper
pumpkins, cornstalks, or fall leaf prints to add to the stage
set-up.

Actors Reception

If time allows, hold a reception for the cast and audience—
serve pumpkin pie and apple juice, of course! If you like,
follow the reception with pumpkin carving.

Elf Collar Party Wear

Materials: Silver tinsel, red construction paper, scissors, stapler, glue, brushes

Preparation: Cut a long, wide strip of construction paper for each child, long enough so that it will slip easily over the child's head and rest on the shoulders like a collar when the ends meet. Cut the tinsel into short, odd lengths. Encourage the children to dress in bright holiday colors for the party.

Activity: Have the children fold the strip of red paper in half lengthwise. Then tell them to spread the inside of the folded strip with glue, then press shut. Next, let them spread liberal amounts of glue all over one side of the strip. Have them press on lots of tinsel pieces and let dry. Staple the ends of the paper strips together and help the children slip on their glittering Christmas collars. *Note:* This is a messy craft! The activity will work best if the children press down a lot of tinsel at once.

Elf Bells

Materials: Yarn or string, jingle bells, scissors

Preparation: Cut short lengths of yarn or string.

Activity: Have the children thread the yarn through the bells and attach them to their shoes for jingly walking and play.

Party Table Decorations

Materials: Several colors of glitter, white sheet, white pillow cases, bonded polyester batting, silver tinsel, sequins or stars, jumbo-size cotton balls, yarn, brushes, glue, pins

Preparation: Ask the children to help create an all-white winter wonderland motif for your Christmas party by each bringing a white pillow case from home.

Activity: Add a tablecloth to the party table by covering it with a white sheet. Have the children cover the back of each chair with a white pillow case. Then tie bunches of tinsel together with yarn and pin a bunch to the back of each chair. Roll out a strip of bonded polyester batting for a table runner and encourage the children to use the brushes and glue to paint on stars, trees, ribbons and bows, and so on. Let the class sprinkle glitter and sequins or stars on the table runner for a sparkling effect. The children can also glue together stacked cotton balls to make snowmen, and set them around the table.

Star and Snowflake Decorations

Materials: White construction paper, scissors, newspaper, glue bottles, glitter, hole punch, yarn

Preparation: Cut sheets of white paper into star shapes. Make large snowflakes by folding sheets of paper several times and then cutting into the edges with scissors. Cut lengths of yarn for hanging.

Activity: Lay the snowflake and star shapes on newspaper. Then have the children drizzle on glue straight from the squeeze bottles. Let the children sprinkle on glitter. When the shapes have dried, punch a hole in each, tie on a length of yarn, and hang the sparkling stars and snowflakes all around the room.

Snowy Christmas Tree Party Favors

Materials: Clear plastic cups, cotton balls, sequins and stars, gold thread, tiny shiny beads, glue, brushes, marker, bowls, small bags, a few carrots, jingle bells, small treats and favors such as erasers, small rubber animals, stickers, candies, nuts, raisins

Preparation: Distribute cups, brushes, bowls of glue, and bowls of cotton balls. Set out short lengths of gold thread and the sequins and stars. Out of sight of the children, put several treats into a bag for each child.

Activity: Have the children gently fluff several cotton balls. Then have them spread the surface of their cup with glue and press on the cotton to create a snowy Christmas tree. Next they may gently add droplets of glue to certain spots and sprinkle on some of the sparkly decorations. Let the Christmas trees dry. Put each child's name inside the tree. Later, place the trees on the party table. Then tell the children that Santa will make a secret visit to leave treats under their trees. Put a few carrots outside for Santa's reindeer. Then have an adult keep the children busy in another room while you hide a small bag of treats under each child's tree. Shake some large jingle bells and give a deep "Ho, Ho, Ho!" before leaving the room; be sure to eat or remove some of the carrots as evidence that Santa and his reindeer were indeed there!

Cookie Cutter Sandwich Snacks

Materials: White sandwich bread, extra large metal Christmas cookie cutters, thinly sliced lunch meats and cheeses, paper plates, plastic knives, mayonnaise and mustard

Preparation: Spread bread slices with a thin layer of mayo and mustard. Place the slices, spread side down, on a clean cutting surface.

Activity: Have the children decide which cookie cutter shape they would like to use for their sandwich. Then have them press the cutter firmly and quickly into two bread slices. Let the children turn their shaped slices over and make a sandwich with the meat and cheese of their choice. Serve on paper plates.

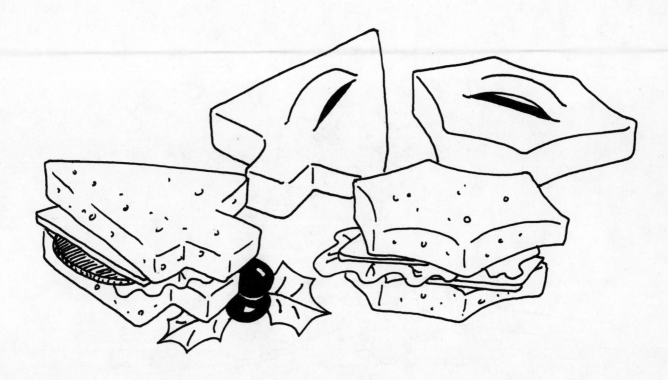

Pin the Star on the Christmas Tree Game

Materials: Large piece of green poster board, yellow and other bright colors of construction paper, scissors, glue, tacks, tape

Preparation: Cut out a large, wide, leafy Christmas tree from the poster board. Cut a large yellow paper star for each child and back the stars with tape.

Activity: Let the children cut out ornaments from the colored paper in a variety of shapes. Tack up the tree at child height and let the children glue the ornaments on. Then, one at a time, blindfold the children, give them a few spins, and have them try to press their star to the top of the tree.

Hanukkah Candle Hat Party Wear

Materials: Plain white paper plates, blue and yellow construction paper, scissors, glue

Preparation: Cut the center out of each paper plate to fashion a crown, first inverting one plate on a child's head to check for size. Cut out eight finger-size or shorter blue paper strips and one slightly larger blue strip for each child. Bend the bottom edges of these candles. Cut out nine small yellow flames for each child.

Activity: First let the children glue a yellow flame to the straight end of each blue candle. Let dry a few minutes. Then have the children glue the bent ends of the candles all along the front edge of the hat. Put the large candle at one end.

Egg Carton Menorah Decorations

Materials: Cardboard egg cartons, clay, small pipe cleaners, glitter, scissors, glue, brushes

Preparation: Cut the top off the egg cartons and discard. Cut away the last three egg sections from one end of each carton. Cut the pipe cleaners in half.

Activity: Have the children roll up balls of clay large enough to secure the pipe cleaners and insert one ball firmly into each section of their carton. Next let the children brush liberal amounts of glue all around the outside edges of the carton and along the top of the section dividers. Then have them sprinkle on colorful glitter. Finally, have them gently press a pipe cleaner half into each of the balls of clay.

Hanukkah Paper Chain Decorations

Materials: Blue and white construction paper, scissors, glue

Preparation: Cut the blue and white paper into short, wide strips.

Activity: Show the children how to fold a paper strip over and glue the ends together. Then have each child make a paper chain, slipping a strip through each ring and securing the ends. Have the children alternate blue and white rings, the traditional Hanukkah colors. Hang the festive chains across doorways or windows.

Hanukkah Gelt Party Favors

Materials: Yellow construction paper, Hanukkah gelt (either pennies or the traditional holiday gold foil-wrapped chocolate coins), glitter, scissors, marker, glue, stapler (optional)

Preparation: Outline the pattern below onto folded pieces of yellow construction paper, enough to give one to each child. Cut out, making sure not to cut the solid line along the fold. Let the children do the cutting if they are able.

Activity: Let the children spread glue along the outside edges of the paper circles and decorate with glitter. Let dry. Collect the decorated circles and, out of sight, place a real or chocolate coin inside. Staple or glue the edges shut. Hide the Hanukkah gelt about the room, then let the children search for their prize!

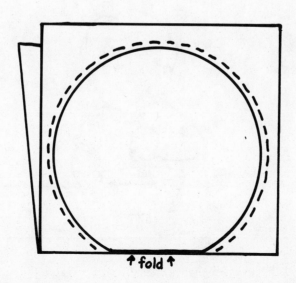

↑ fold ↑

Potato Latkes Snacks

Materials: 3 large peeled potatoes, 2 tablespoons flour, 1 small onion, 1 teaspoon salt, pepper to taste, 2 beaten eggs, 1/2 cup oil, grater, large bowl, spoon, slotted spoon, frying pan, paper towels, spatula

Preparation: Coarsely grate the potatoes. Finely grate the onion and add to potatoes. Add beaten eggs (allow the children to help beat them), flour, salt, and pepper. Stir, then let sit ten minutes to thicken. Press with a slotted spoon and pour off excess liquid. Heat the oil to medium or medium high in the frying pan.

Activity: Drop the mixture by tablespoonfuls into the oil. Fry the pancakes until lightly brown and crispy at the edges, then turn. Remove and blot on paper towels. Serve warm. Makes 16 to 18 latkes.

Dreidel Spinning Game

Materials: Pencil, lightweight cardboard, marker, scissors, munchies such as raisins, popcorn, or pretzels

Preparation: Create your own traditional dreidel by cutting a three- or four-inch square from the cardboard. Divide the square into four sections by marking it diagonally from corner to corner. In each section put one of the letters N, G, H, or S. Poke a small hole in the center with the scissors, then slip the square onto the pencil (see the illustration).

Activity: Give each player the same number of munchies. Have each player put two in the pot to start the game. Tell the first player to place the dreidel pencil point down on the table and spin it. The letter it lands on indicates what to do: N—Player does nothing, next player spins; G—Player takes all that's in the pot, other players put one munchie in the pot to get it going again; H—Player takes half of what's in the pot; S—Player must put one munchie in the pot. Whenever the pot is empty or there is just one item left, have all the players put one in to fill the pot up again before the next spin. Play ends when one player has won everything or, for younger children, when each player has taken a pre-determined number of spins. Keep extra munchies on hand for after-game snacking.

Chinese New Year Parade

The Chinese New Year arrives with the second new moon following the winter solstice. Many modern Chinese have adopted the custom of celebrating the New Year on the first day of January, but they still keep the treasured customs handed down from their ancestors. Festivities can last up to two weeks and are centered in the home. Take a cue from the traditional celebration and prepare for the New Year and the Festival of Lanterns in the following ways.

Super Sweep: Get out the dust mops, brooms, and brushes and have the children help you tidy the room: the Chinese have traditionally cleaned every nook and cranny in anticipation of the New Year celebration. If any old dust is left behind on the New Year, it's believed to be bad luck.

Lucky Red: To the Chinese, the color red represents good luck and happiness. Hang scrolls of red paper about the room with wishes for harmony and prosperity. Arrange flowers, a sign of growth, in pretty, artful presentations. Use red flowers if available.

Festival of Lanterns: The New Year celebration ends with a parade of lanterns led by a huge dragon, the symbol of strength and goodness. The dragon is usually very long with many men hidden inside to carry its colorful, wriggling shape through the streets. Let each child live the fantasy by wearing the dragon costumes and carrying the lanterns that follow. Parade watchers can bang pans and shake rattles.

Traditional Paper Lanterns

Materials: Bright construction paper, yarn, ruler, marker, stapler, scissors, hole punch, binder hole reinforcers

Preparation: Fold a sheet of construction paper in half lengthwise. Mark the paper as shown in the illustration. Cut lengths of yarn.

Activity: Show the children how to cut into the folded edge of the paper and cut along the lines just until they meet the line across the top. When they are done cutting, have the children unfold the paper, bring the short sides together, and staple at top and bottom. Punch a hole on each side and let the children press on hole reinforcers. String the lanterns with yarn.

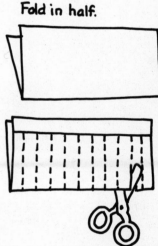

Fold in half.

33

Dragon Costumes

Materials: Large paper grocery bags, pieces of colorful or metallic fabric, crepe paper, scissors, paint, brushes, glue, stapler, face paint (optional)

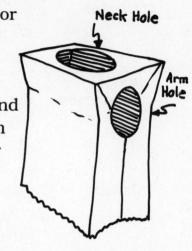

Preparation: Measure a child and then cut a head hole and two armholes in each bag. Have the children try the bags on for size. Cut the crepe paper into long streamers.

Activity: Allow the children to glue or staple colorful fabric shapes to the back of their bag. Have them paint a dragon's face or a colorful design on the front of the bag. Let the bags dry. Help the children staple streamers over the armholes. If you wish, use the face paints to give the children a fierce dragon look. Then let the children carefully slip their dragon costumes on, carry the lanterns they made, and parade in a line all around the school.

Broken Heart Party Wear

Materials: Sheets of red construction paper, scissors, safety pins or masking tape, clear tape

Preparation: Cut out one large red paper heart for each child. Cut the hearts in half, each in a different, distinctive way. Give one half of a heart to each child to pin or tape on. Hide all the other halves throughout the room or play area.

Activity: At some point during the day, instruct the children to go hunting for the other half of their broken heart. Let them take off their heart halves and hold them while they hunt. When they spy a heart half, they may go to it quietly and see if it matches. If it doesn't match, they should leave it and hunt for another. If the heart does match, give the child some tape for mending and then have the child pin the mended heart back on.

Tunnel of Love Decoration

Materials: Refrigerator box or several smaller boxes, bright paints, brushes

Activity: Lay an old refrigerator box on its side or line up several smaller boxes end to end to form a tunnel. Allow the children to help paint the outside of the boxes with bright hearts and flowers. Place the Tunnel of Love at the entrance to the party area and have the children crawl through it to enter.

Heart Place Mats

Materials: Large sheets of red construction paper, scissors, glue, glitter, stickers, paper doilies, gold and silver yarn or thick thread, marker

Activity: Show the children how to fold a sheet of construction paper in half and then cut it to create a heart shape. Set out glue and the decorative materials listed and allow the children to embellish their place mats. Let the mats dry, label them with the children's name, and place them at the party table.

Love Bug Party Favors

Materials: Hinged wooden clothespins, red felt, googly eyes, tiny pink pompons, scissors, marker, glue

Preparation: Cut out enough small felt hearts so there is one for each child.

Activity: Have the children glue a heart to the top of the pinching end of their clothespin. Let dry for a few moments. Then have the children glue on a pompon nose and two googly eyes. Write each child's name on the bottom of his or her clothespin. The love bugs can be used to hold name cards at the party table or to carry a handmade card to a special friend or Valentine.

To my Valentine

Pink Peppermint Patties Snacks

Materials: Plain chocolate wafers, 1-pound can of ready-to-serve vanilla frosting, hard peppermint candies (wrapped), 1/2 tsp. peppermint extract, red food coloring, bowl, stirring spoon, wooden mallet, plastic knives, serving tray

Preparation: Empty the frosting into the bowl. Add the peppermint extract and blend well.

Activity: Allow the children to take turns with the mallet and hammer the wrapped candies a few times so that they are broken into small bits (use as many candies as you need for your class size). Then have the children unwrap the candies and shake the bits into the bowl of frosting. Next, squeeze in six or more drops of red food coloring to create the shade of pink you desire. Let all the children take a turn stirring the frosting. Then give each child a plastic knife and a few wafers. Let the children gently spread on the peppermint frosting, then place the wafers on a serving tray. Serve the pink peppermint sweets at your table.

Lover's Leap Game

Materials: Chalk; paved area for play; small candy hearts, stickers, pencils, or other similar treats

Preparation: On a sidewalk or paved area, use the chalk to draw six large hearts all in a row. Space the hearts far enough apart so that the children can leap from one to the next.

Activity: Have two adults join hands to make a bridge and sing the following rhyme to the tune of "London Bridge Is Falling Down":

Lovers leaping, hopping 'round,
Hopping 'round, hopping 'round!
Lovers leaping, hopping 'round,
My dear sweetheart!

Let the children walk around and under the bridge until one is caught on "My dear sweetheart!" That child goes to the row of hearts and leaps from heart to heart as everyone chants, counting out the six hearts. Give the child one of the prizes at the end. Then have the child re-enter the game and start up play again.

Every Bunny Needs Some Bunny Play

Act 1

Narrator: Valentine's Day was very near, and all the bunnies in the forest were busy and excited. They hopped about the forest floor, collecting flowers for their sweethearts. One little bunny, Billy Bunny, especially loved Valentine's Day.

(Several bunnies hop around the stage, some holding pink tissue flowers, others admiring their pink paper hearts. The bunnies pause as Billy Bunny hops toward the front of the stage holding a large pink heart.)

Billy Bunny: I love Valentine's Day! Pink, pink, pink!

Narrator: (interrupting just as Billy Bunny is finishing): I wonder if Billy Bunny has a favorite <u>color</u>?

All other bunnies: (turning toward the audience and shouting): PINK!

(Billy Bunny and the other bunnies begin to hop around again.)

Narrator: Yes, it was the day before Valentine's Day, a wonderful day—until a storm began to brew... and brew...

(Clouds and Lightning Bolts stomp their feet, lightly at first and then harder and harder.)

Narrator: ...and brew until it burst! The thunder clapped!

(Clouds clap loudly.)

The lightning crackled!

(Lightning Bolts shake pieces of heavy aluminum foil.)

Narrator: And the rain came pouring down. But it was so cold the rain quickly turned to snow.

(Clouds throw cotton balls around the stage. Billy runs around, trying to hide. The other bunnies run offstage. In the confusion, Billy drops his paper heart.)

Narrator: The storm raged around Billy. Soon he cried out when he saw that his heart was gone.

Billy Bunny: My heart!! My heart!

Narrator and all bunnies offstage: (singing to the familiar tune):

> It's snowing, it's snowing,
> The snowstorm is blowing.
> Billy Bunny bumped his head and
> Didn't get up 'til morning.

(While searching for his heart, Billy Bunny bumps his head against a log and falls asleep.)

Narrator: (to audience): Now, close your eyes as Billy's done. Open them when the bell has rung.

(Draw curtain if there is one.)

Act 2

(Curtain opens and/or a bell rings. The stage is covered with cotton balls. Billy Bunny is just beginning to wake up, rubbing his head.)

Narrator: When Billy Bunny finally woke up, the storm had passed. But all Billy's friends were gone.

Billy Bunny: I'm scared. Where is everyone?

Narrator: Cupid was nearby for Valentine's Day, and saw that Billy was sad. So Cupid told Billy that everything would be all right.

(Cupid enters, tossing flowers all about, sneaks up behind Billy, and gives him a hug. Then Cupid sits down next to Billy, who cries on Cupid's shoulder for a moment. Soon Cupid dries Billy's tears with a hankie.)

Narrator: The day had not started well for Billy Bunny. But the storm was over, the clouds all went away, and a blazing sun began to shine.

(Clouds place a large sun on the stage and crouch behind it. Billy and Cupid get up, clasp hands, and turn in a circle.)

Narrator: Billy Bunny and Cupid began to play in the sunshine. They were dancing and playing when Cupid found Billy's pink heart.

(Cupid hands the heart to Billy.)

Billy Bunny: My pink heart!

(Billy drops to his knees, closes his eyes, and holds the heart to his chest.)

Narrator: Billy <u>loves</u> pink!

Billy Bunny: Pink...pink...pink...

Narrator: But soon Billy Bunny frowned. He wished he could give his valentine heart to another little bunny. Cupid decided to find Billy a friend.

(Cupid comes over to Billy and starts to whisper in his ear.)

Narrator: Just then, Cupid gave Billy Bunny a nice big pinch on the arm. It made Billy fall in love—with Bonnie Bunny!

(Cupid pinches Billy. At the same time, Bonnie Bunny comes hopping onto the stage.)

Narrator: Bonnie Bunny was a picture of spring, a picture of happiness, a picture of...

All bunnies offstage: PINK!

(Bonnie Bunny hops up to Billy.)

Narrator: Billy Bunny gave Bonnie his heart, and from that day on Billy and Bonnie were the best of friends.

(Billy gives Bonnie his pink heart, and the two hold hands facing the audience. All the other bunnies and other characters come back onto the stage.)

Narrator: And it all goes to show that...

Entire cast: Every <u>bunny</u> needs some <u>bunny</u>!

Stage Set-Up

This play can be performed outside or you can decorate an inside area to look like the edge of a forest or meadow. Scatter plenty of sticks, firewood, or driftwood about the edges of an area to create stage boundaries. Potted plants and wildflowers on a low table and grass or weeds strewn about create a woodsy atmosphere.

On the left of the stage, place a card table covered with a brown blanket and weeds and grass for a bunny den, or let the children make a bunny den by painting a large cardboard box. Rig a curtain or partition so that the den exits offstage. Have one or two clouds stand on the rear right of the stage with one or two lightning bolts sitting on low footstools in front of them. If indoors, you may want to decorate the curtain and walls with pink paper hearts, streamers, and balloons.

Characters

Billy Bunny	Bonnie Bunny
Clouds (1 or 2)	Lightning Bolts (1 or 2)
Baby Bunnies (any number)	Cupid

Costumes

Billy Bunny should wear a white shirt and pants, or as close to all white clothes as possible, or, if the actor prefers, all black clothes or all brown clothes. Billy should also wear a matching bunny ear headband made by gluing a pipe cleaner between two paper bunny ear shapes (make two ears) and taping the ears to a plastic headband. Bonnie Bunny should wear all pink clothes, and a pink bunny ear headband like the one for Billy Bunny. Baby bunnies wear bunny ear headbands and all white, all black, or all brown clothes.

Cupid should dress in bright multi-colored clothes, and have flowers or greenery in his or her hair. Pin on lots of pink paper hearts. Cupid also needs to carry a handkerchief. The clouds should be draped in white sheets with a cloud-shaped piece of foam batting pinned to the front. Have the lightning bolts wear black or dark-colored clothes with pieces of foil sticking out from the pockets, sleeves, and neckline. Make a lightweight cardboard cloud and paste on zig-zag lightning bolts. String the cloud with ribbon or heavy yarn and hang it from the shoulders.

Props

In addition to costume and stage materials you will need pink tissue paper flowers (simply twist ends of paper together and secure with tape), lots of pink paper hearts, a bag or two of cotton balls for the clouds to throw, a bell, and a large cardboard sun painted yellow.

Silly Party Wear

Materials: Oversized shirts and shoes, silly floppy hats or pointy party hats, old socks, mittens, face paints, and other similar items, or just let the children create April Fool's Day wear from what they have on

Activity: Let the children do everything upside down and backwards on April Fool's Day, including dressing. Have the children wear shoes on the wrong feet or trade shoes and socks and wear a mismatched pair! They can put shirts on backwards, wear socks on their hands, or put mittens on their feet. They can also create silly faces with face paints or wear pointy party hats sticking off the back of their head or out from their forehead. Silliness is the dress of the day!

Upside-Down and Backwards Decorations

Materials: Tape, tacks, scissors, glue, old magazines, crepe paper streamers, toilet paper, colorful newspaper comic sections, balloons, other colorful materials

Activity: Let the children's imagination run wild as they think of silly, nonsensical ways to decorate and rearrange the room. Let them hang shoes from the ceiling, turn lamp shades upside down, re-hang posters and pictures upside down, and turn clocks to the wrong time. They can decorate with colorful crepe paper streamers or drape the room with toilet paper for a totally silly effect. Dozens of balloons can be scattered about the floor. When the table is set, use newspaper comic sections for place mats, turn plates and cups upside down, and hide napkins under plates. The children may also want to cut in half animal pictures from nature magazines, then glue different animal halves together. They can also cut up pictures of food or people and glue them together incorrectly. Hang these silly pictures all about the room.

Smiley Surprise Party Favors

Materials: Colorful party blowers, white lightweight cardboard or poster board, thick black marker, glitter, star stickers, glue, crayons, tiny pink or red pompons (optional), scissors or craft knife

Preparation: Copy the illustration below onto cardboard and cut out. Outline with heavy black marker. At the center of the mouth make several cuts diagonally across one another, then poke a finger through to open the hole, pushing through from the front to the back.

Activity: First let the children decorate the smiley surprises. They may wish to color the mouth bright red and then outline with glue and glitter, color the nose a funny color, or press on some stars. When they're through, show them how to push the mouthpiece of the blower through the hole in the smile. Children can hold up their smiley surprises and blow into the party favor for a silly April Fool's Day greeting!

Inside-Out and Peanut Butter Surprise Sandwich Snacks

Materials: Cheese or lunch meat slices; sandwich bread; mayonnaise and/or mustard; peanut butter; sandwich spread toppings such as raisins, thin fruit slices, shredded coconut, and finely chopped dried fruit; plastic knives; bowls

Preparation: Put all the ingredients out on a low table.

Activity: Let the children create their own inside-out sandwiches by spreading mayo or mustard on a slice of bread and then "sandwiching" it between two slices of cheese or lunch meat. The children can create their own fun and surprising alternatives to the standard PB and J sandwich by spreading peanut butter on one side of a slice of bread and then sprinkling on one of the toppings above. *Note:* If you serve a beverage with the sandwiches, you may want to use Crazy Straws, or Twisty Straws, for more April Fool's Day fun.

Non-Musical Chairs Game

Materials: One chair for each child, music

Preparation: Set up the chairs in a traditional Musical
Chairs circle.

Activity: Play Musical Chairs a bit backwards: Have the
children walk around the chairs while there is
no music playing, then rush to sit in a chair
when the music starts. Let everyone find a
seat for the first round, then remove a chair
each round.

Relay Race Game

Activity: Hold a number of running and walking relays
of your own creation, but have team members
run and walk backwards, of course!

Pass the Silly Face Game

Activity: Start the game by having one child make a
crazy face to the child on his or her right. That
child catches the silly face and passes it to the
next child. Let play continue all around the
circle, then let a new child begin passing a
different silly face.

Easter Parade

The idea of wearing something new, such as a bright bonnet, on Easter is not new. In ancient times it was thought that wearing a new article of clothing on the New Year, which was always celebrated in spring, would bring good luck to the wearer for the next twelve months. In the more recent past the traditional Easter parade down New York's Fifth Avenue drew only influential and wealthy citizens wearing the finest fashions. The ladies were sure to wear a striking new bonnet and hoop skirt and the men to carry a gold-knobbed cane. Present-day Easter parades now offer the chance for everyone to promenade wearing everything from fine fashions to outlandish costumes. Your students can hold their own very special parade by using some of the following ideas.

Costumes

Follow the directions for the bonnets and boutonnieres that follow for the children to wear during the parade. The children may also create and wear their own Easter finery, which may include gloves and walking sticks. Have the children wear their costumes along the parade route you select.

Music

Try to find a copy of the old standard "The Easter Parade," ca. 1933, by Irving Berlin, for parade accompaniment. Otherwise use any music that inspires an elegant gait or puts a lively spring in the step!

Easter Bonnets

Materials: Small bright-colored plastic bowls (use a size that will fit on the children's heads), colored tissue paper, old gift-wrapping bows, shredded foil, old artificial flowers, bits of ribbon and lace, elastic, glue, stapler, scissors

Preparation: Measure a length of elastic and then staple it to both sides of the inside edge of the bowls; this will be the chin strap. Cut tissue into flower shapes, saving scraps. Set out all the materials.

Activity: Let the children create their very own millinery designs by gluing tissue flowers, scraps, bows, and artificial flowers to the top of the inverted bowl in any way they wish. Encourage the children to embellish their hats extravagantly. Let dry. Have the children wear their hats for proud promenading!

Easter Boutonnieres

Materials: Coffee filters, stapler, glue, pins, old wrapping bows, shredded foil, old artificial flowers, bits of ribbon and lace, scissors

Preparation: Stack together three or four coffee filters for each child and staple in the center to secure. Set out all the materials.

Activity: Let the children glue bits of the decorative materials to the center of their filters, creating a small bouquet to wear on their shirt. If old artificial flowers are used, make sure they are lightweight so the coffee filter base can support them. Let dry. Pin the boutonnieres on at parade time.

Floppy Bunny Ears Party Wear

Materials: Two white paper plates for each child; pink, brown, and black crayons; stapler; scissors

Preparation: Fold in half one paper plate for each child and cut out enough of the center so the hat will fit securely atop the child's head.

Activity: Have the children cut their other paper plate evenly in half. Then have them trim each half into an ear shape (help them if necessary). Next, let the children color the center of the ears pink, brown, black, or spotted. Fold the bottom edges of the ears down, then help the children staple the ears to either side of the plate.

Paper Plate Bunny Decorations

Materials: Two white paper plates for each child, pink yarn, crayons, marker, scissors, glue, tacks

Preparation: Cut the yarn into short lengths. Outline one plate for each child as shown in the illustration below. Give each child one plain and one outlined plate.

Activity: Have the children cut the plate apart along the lines. If they wish, they may color the ear pieces any color they like. They may also color in eyes and nose on the plain plate and then glue on some yarn whiskers. To assemble, have the children attach the two ears to the top edge of the face with liberal amounts of glue. The bow tie should be glued to the bottom edge. Let the bunnies dry completely and then tack them up for display.

Big-Eared Bunny Party Favors

Materials: Toilet paper tubes, cotton balls, white or pastel-colored yarn, crayons or markers, scissors, glue, snack or treat mix

Preparation: First cut a V on both sides of one end of a tube for each child (see the illustration). Round off the edges if desired. Cut the yarn into short lengths.

Activity: Show the children how to use a marker or crayon to make two pink eyes on their tube. Then have them color on a nose and glue on yarn whiskers. Direct them to glue a fluffy cotton ball tail to the back of the tube. Let dry completely. Label the bunnies with the children's names, then place them on the party table and fill with treats. *Note:* The children can use these bunnies as finger puppets with material in the Easter section of *Holiday Hoopla: Songs and Finger Plays.*

56

Bird's Nest Cupcake Snacks

Materials: One package any flavor cake mix, muffin tins or paper baking cups, white or pastel-colored frosting, shredded coconut, jelly beans, green food coloring, plastic knives, bowls, mixing spoon, jar

Preparation: Prepare the cake mix, giving each child a chance to stir. Let the children count out their stirring strokes, then pass the bowl to the next person. Bake the cupcakes as directed on the package. Let cool. Place coconut in a jar, add a few drops of green food coloring, and shake until evenly tinted. Place the frosting and coconut in several small bowls. Put out the knives and jelly beans.

Activity: Allow each child to frost his or her own cupcake. Then show the children how to sprinkle on some green coconut to make a fluffy nest in the center. Finally, let them choose three jelly beans, naming the colors as they choose, and place these "eggs" in the nest.

Easter Basket Game

Materials: A plain hard-boiled egg for each child, one red egg, one blue egg, one green egg, a basket

Preparation: Have the entire group sit in a circle. Choose one child to be the bunny. Tell the bunny to sit in the center of the circle holding the basket and hiding his or her eyes.

Activity: At random, give either a plain or a colored egg to each child in the circle. Place any extra plain eggs in the basket. Then have the children pass their eggs all around the circle while they sing this song, concealing the eggs from view on the last line:

A tisket, a tasket, a pretty Easter basket.
I saw a bunny in the grass,
I want the eggs he's hiding, he's hiding!

A green one, a blue one, a red one for my
  basket.
I saw a bunny in the grass,
I want the eggs he's hiding, he's hiding!

After the song, tell the bunny to open his or her eyes and ask for a red, blue, or a green egg for the basket. The child holding that egg drops it in the basket and becomes the bunny. The first bunny joins the circle, taking the colored egg along, and the game continues.

Baldric Party Wear

Materials: Wide green ribbon, green fabric, or green crepe paper; scissors; safety pins (optional)

Preparation: Baldrics, or sashes that go over the right shoulder and tie at the waist, originally were worn by celebrants in ancient times. For your May Day celebrants, cut the green ribbon, cloth, or crepe paper into long lengths (crepe paper is very inexpensive but won't be as durable).

Activity: Either attach the baldrics with a pin at the shoulder and waist, or cut longer lengths that will go over both front *and* back and tie at the waist. Let the children wear their sashes for the party and Maypole play.

Maypole Hats

Materials: Pointed party hats, fresh or artificial flowers and greenery, narrow ribbon, scissors, tape

Preparation: If possible, let the children gather flowers, leaves, and other greenery from an outdoor area. Otherwise, set the materials out on a table. Use the scissors to snip off the tops of the party hats.

Activity: Have the children select the flowers and leaves they wish to use and gently poke them into the hole at the top of the hat. They may wish to add a few lengths of ribbon as well. Then help the children reach into the hat from the underside and secure the flowers with tape. The hat is now a wearable version of a Maypole!

Maypole Decorations

Materials: Large stake, tree, or beach umbrella; basket; ivy, fronds, or other greenery; fresh flowers of all sorts or artificial and paper flowers; vinyl duct tape or tacks; lightweight rope; scissors; colorful crepe paper streamers; hammer (optional); bucket of sand (optional)

Preparation: Tell the children that, traditionally, in the spring, a large tree was cut from the forest, stripped of its branches, and then erected in the center of the village for a Maypole. Their Maypole, however, will be constructed in a more simple way. Have the children help you collect Maypole greenery and flowers and make an abundant arrangement in a basket.

Activity: If there is a tree in the center of a clearing or play area, simply hang the May basket from a limb, then decorate the rest of the tree with streamers. Or take a large stake and tack or tape streamers to the top. Hammer the stake into the ground and hook the basket over the top. Let the children play with the streamers, twining and twisting them around the pole. Or poke a beach umbrella into a five-gallon bucket of sand. Tape streamers around the edge of the umbrella so they hang down. Fill the bucket with flowers and greenery. This last idea works well for a rainy day celebration.

Mini-Maypole Party Favors

Materials: Empty thread spools (be sure the holes are large enough to fit a straw through), three different-colored pastel pipe cleaners per child, straws, small bunches of artificial flowers, construction paper, pipe cleaners, scissors, glue

Preparation: If the paper label on one end of each spool is not intact, cut a small circle of paper and glue it to the bottom. If the flower bunches you're using come in a large bunch (flowers used for bridal favors usually contain eight or nine separate tiny bunches), separate them and trim the stems slightly. Cut the pipe cleaners in half.

Activity: First have the children insert a straw into the spool (the paper circle will prevent the straw from poking through). Then have them insert the pipe cleaners, one at a time, about a third of the way into the straw and then bend down. Next, let them select a tiny bunch of flowers and insert it into the straw, pushing the stem all the way in so that flowers sit on the top of the straw. The mini-Maypoles can be party favors or make great tabletop decorations.

Green Apple Sweets Snacks

Materials: Thinly sliced green apples, lightly sweetened whipping cream, green food coloring, wire whisk, bowls, mixing spoon

Preparation: Tell the children that May Day has traditionally been celebrated by feasting on green foods to celebrate the greenery of the season. Allow the children to take turns whipping the cream with a wire whisk. When the cream is ready, add just a few drops of the food coloring, drop by drop, until a nice shade of green appears.

Activity: Let each child take several apple slices and dip them in the green cream for a fun finger food.

Ring Around the Maypole Game

Preparation: Gather the children in a circle around the Maypole. Ask them to hold hands, dance around, and sing this song to the tune of "Ring Around the Rosie."

Activity: Ring around the Maypole, a pocketful of posies!
May Day! May Day! We all fall down!

Add your own variations, such as, "We all jump high!" or "We all turn around!" *Note: Other Maypole songs are included in Holiday Hoopla: Songs and Finger Plays.*

Circus Parade

Materials: Face paint, crepe paper, crayons, scissors, glue, tape, stapler, safety pins, string, pieces of fabric, props, clothing and costumes from home (see suggestions below for characters and props).

Animals: Use face paints to create animal faces. Ask the children to dress in colors that suit their animal, such as brown or black for a bear, orange for a lion, and gray for an elephant. Attach fabric tails with pins.

Clowns: Use face paints to create funny clown faces. Have the children dress in oversized clothing, funny ties, and floppy hats. (Be sure, though, that they wear safe, comfortable shoes.) Blow up balloons for the clowns to carry or let the children tie lengths of string to small toys or trinkets to hand out to people along the parade route.

Acrobats: Have these children wear leotards and tights or other close-fitting clothes. Add sparkly accents such as beads, a rhinestone sash, or colorful netting. The acrobats can carry long scarves or batons to jump and twirl with.

Trainers: Animal trainers can dress in all black and wear gloves and a big buckled belt. The children can carry Hula-Hoops or a long belt or stick for a whip.

Strong Man /Woman: Muscle builders can wear tights or dark pants and a long-sleeved shirt. Have them stuff crumpled newspaper or toilet paper into their clothing to simulate muscles.

Musicians: Musicians can wear bright clothing and hats. They can bring toy instruments such as tambourines and drums from home, or create dazzling trumpets by covering paper towel tubes with colored paper and gluing on long crepe paper streamers. Have the children hum loudly through the trumpets as they march.

Vendors: Food vendors should wear bright or striped clothing. To make vending boxes, staple a long strap to small, shallow boxes. Fill the boxes with bags of popcorn, peanuts, raisins, or penny candy and have the children wear the boxes hung over their shoulders. The vendors can hand out treats along the parade route or at the post-parade introductions.

Bicycle Acrobats: Children love to parade on their bikes or trikes so provide crepe paper and streamers to attach to the wheels. Clip cards to the wheels for a noisy parade.

Wagon Drivers: Let children decorate red wagons or other carts from home and fill them with their favorite stuffed animals. Crepe paper streamers can be taped to the wagon sides. The children can also create colorful, sectioned wheels from construction paper and glue them to the wagon wheels. Tin cans or bells tied to the back let everyone know the circus parade is on its way!

Post-Parade Introductions

Preparation: Select a stage area where all the parade characters can wait out of sight. Then act as the narrator and introduce the different parade groups to the audience with the following lines. Encourage applause for each group as the children enter. Give each group an assigned area in which to sit or stand after they receive their applause.

Narrator: When you're at the circus, all these people you will see (extend arm toward entry):

First, the wagons come rumbling and rolling (have the wagon drivers enter pulling their cartloads of animals)!

And next the vendors bring treats for you and for me (have the food vendors enter passing out popcorn and treats)!

And now the musicians get the circus show rolling (have the musicians enter humming, blowing, and drumming loudly)!

The acrobats twirl and hop, entertaining us all (have the acrobats enter cartwheeling and prancing)!

The clowns are clumsy and silly, and always seem to fall (have the clowns enter, stumbling over one another and falling in a heap)!

And finally the brave men and women who train the beasts (have the trainers enter, holding up hoops; have the wagon drivers enter and throw stuffed animals through the hoops)!

Circus Game

Materials: Small drum, Hula-Hoops, ropes, different-sized balls, footstool, board for balancing, paper-covered barrel for a cannon, jungle gym play area or lawn area

Preparation: Check your library for circus music to use in the background. Prepare a list of circus tricks you will call for.

Activity: To the accompaniment of a drum roll, use the dramatic voice of a circus ringmaster and announce the following or similar stunts. Encourage the children to take part in the stunts, and serve them circus animal crackers after they have performed. The children will love it if you keep up the dramatic suspense.

"And now, a stunt never seen before in this country, a double-loop cartwheel!"

"Hold onto your hats, ladies and gentlemen! The Flying Fandangoes will now jump from the high wire footstool and land on both feet!"

"See the seal balance a ball on his head while sneezing!"

"See the ferocious, lumbering brown bear jump through the hoop!"

"Jumbo, the gigantic elephant, will now balance on one leg!"

"And now, the death-defying daredevils walk the balancing board high above!"

"Will the amazing Human Cannonball survive a blast through the air?"

Japanese Star Festival (Tannabata) Story

The Japanese Star Festival, held in early July, began as a celebration of the ancient legend of Altair and Vega. Farmers made offerings of food and women made offerings of cloth; children wrote romantic poems. Children today still create poems on colorful paper. Tell your children the following story of Altair and Vega; they can act out the story in the mini-play at the end of this section.

Let us tell a special tale
That's as bright as a starlit trail.
Altair was the Cowherd Star,
Vega was the Weaver Star.
One day these glittering stars above
Met and fell so much in love.
They decided to go off to play,
And forgot their work from day to day.
"Vega should be weaving!" shouted the Heavenly King.
"And Altair's always leaving—he's a playful thing!"
So the Heavenly King sent them apart.
This broke the stars' hearts.
But on the seventh day of the seventh moon
It was told that Vega could see her friend soon.
But to find Altair on that night,
She had to cross the sky and forget her fright.
Alone and afraid, she had to cross the Milky Way,
So the magpies made a bridge that day!
Up, up, up into the night they flew,
And together their wings made a bridge like new!
Vega went across to the one she missed,
And once again the stars kissed!
And so, each and every year,
Vega can see her friend so dear.
But only on the seventh day of the seventh moon.
So she always hopes that day comes soon.
And if it doesn't rain too hard that day,
The magpies' bridge crosses the Milky Way.
So let us hope for clear night skies,
So the stars will meet with the help of the magpies!

Festival Kimonos and Stars Party Wear

Materials: Paper hospital gowns; or paper towels, food coloring, and eye droppers; scissors; fabric scraps; glue; safety pins; yellow construction paper; glitter

Preparation: Ask your local hospital to donate a number of paper hospital gowns. Cut out enough star shapes from the yellow paper to give one to each child.

Activity: Have the children decorate the stars by gluing on bits of colored cloth or glitter. Help the children pin the stars on the hospital-gown kimonos to wear to the Star Festival party. If hospital gowns can't be obtained, let the children use the droppers and food coloring to dye paper towels. A dyed, folded paper towel can act as a broad front sash when attached with a colorful belt. More dyed towel pieces can be tucked in around the children's collars.

Sticker Poem Decorations

Materials: Different colors of construction paper; stickers shaped like stars, flowers, hearts, fruit, and the like; string; scissors; hole punch; binder hole reinforcers; long bamboo poles, dowels, or branches; bamboo fence sections or mats

Preparation: Cut colored paper into strips. Cut string into long lengths.

Activity: Let the children create wishes of good will and love by turning the paper strips into sticker poems. Have them press on stickers, then carefully punch a hole in one end. Help the children reinforce the hole with a binder hole stick-on. Tie several of the poems, spaced in a line, on lengths of string. Attach the strings to poles, branches, bamboo fence sections, or mats.

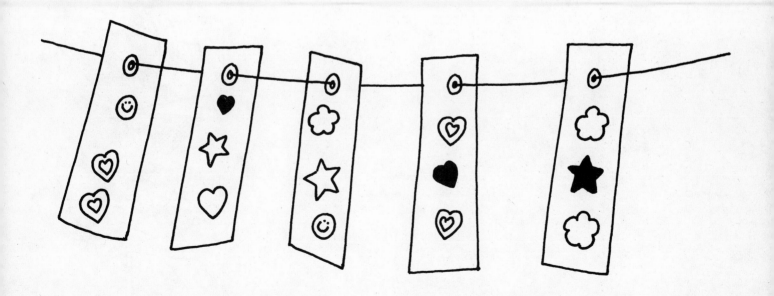

Paper Chains and Flower Decorations

Materials: Different colors of construction paper; scissors; glue or stapler; tape; long bamboo poles, branches, or dowels; different colors of tissue paper

Preparation: Cut the construction paper into strips. Cut the tissue paper into small squares.

Activity: Let the children create simple colorful paper chains by looping the paper strips and gluing or stapling the ends together. Have them create colorful paper flowers by stacking two or three different-colored squares of tissue paper, then drawing up the middle and twisting the center. Show the children how to secure the twisted center with tape and then fluff. Attach the chains and flowers to poles or branches.

Magpie Bridge and Shaped Decorations

Materials: White and other colors of construction paper, glue, scissors, crayons and markers

Preparation: For the magpie cutouts, cut long, wide strips from the white paper and fold them back and forth along the width into a fan. Add markings like those in the illustration. For the shaped cutouts, prepare enough colorful pre-cut shapes of fruits and other foods plus tiny kimonos for the children to decorate (or let them make their own shapes).

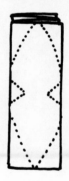

Fold into fan shape.

Activity: To make magpie bridges like the one in the story, have the children use the scissors to cut along the top and bottom lines to trim the ends into pointed wings. Have them make a careful cut on each side of the center almost, but not quite to, the center. Let them unfold their cutouts to see the bridge of magpie wings. To make the shaped decorations, distribute the patterns or shapes or let the children create their own. Have the children decorate the shapes; they may want to glue fruits to leaf shapes or sashes to kimonos. Hang the decorations in the breeze of doorways and windows.

Surprise Star Cup Party Favors

Materials: Small paper cups, yellow construction paper, foil or star stickers, marker, scissors, glue, small favors such as balloons, rubber toys, sticks of gum, jelly beans, bells, erasers, stickers, etc.

Preparation: Trace a star shape on yellow paper for each child. Make the shape large enough to fit over the top of the cup.

Activity: Have the children cut out their star and decorate it by gluing on bits of foil or pressing on stickers. Mark the children's name on their star. Collect the stars and tell the children that their stars will be returned to them as part of a special surprise. Out of the children's sight, fill the cups with treats. Spread glue around the top edge of the cups and press a star on each. Place the cups at the party table for the children to discover their prizes.

Colorful Kimono Party Favors

Materials: Construction paper, scraps of colorful wrapping paper, marker, fabric, colored tissue paper, glue, scissors, colored marking pens, water

Preparation: Outline a simple angular kimono shape on paper for each child.

Activity: Have the children cut out the kimonos, then decorate them by gluing on wrapping paper and fabric scraps. Show the children how to crumple tissue paper and glue it at the center to make a flower sash. Lightly dampen the kimonos and show the children how to color areas with marking pens so the colors bleed.

Fruit Salad Snacks

Materials: Various fruits (have each child bring a piece of fruit from home), whole watermelon, paper plates, scissors, knife

Preparation: See the illustration below for creating a watermelon country basket. Slice two parallel lines across the top to create a handle. Then, out and around from each handle edge, cut jagged slices to give the basket a scalloped look. Carefully lift the pieces out. Hollow out the melon and reserve the fruit.

Activity: Ask the children to help wash the fruit. Then slice the fruit, encouraging the children to name the type and color of all the fruits as you cut. If you have apples, cut them into slices across the width to expose the star pattern made by the seeds. Load the watermelon basket with the fruit. The children can make star plates by cutting points in the edge all around.

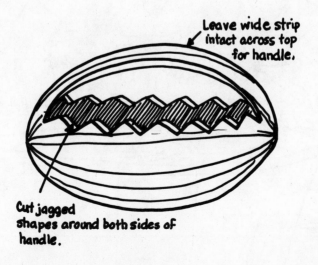

Leave wide strip intact across top for handle.

Cut jagged shapes around both sides of handle.

Ring Around the River Game

Materials: Large tub or play pool full of water, Star Festival paper decorations

Preparation: Have the children circle the pool of water holding the decorations.

Activity: Ask the children to sing this simple song:

Stars around the heavens, shine with love
   tonight!
Send us, send us good luck tonight.
Ring around the river, stars in the sky,
Good luck, good luck, we all say goodbye!

Then end your Star Festival in the traditional way—toss all the paper decorations into the "stream" to bring good luck! Give yourselves a big cheer!

Star Festival Mini-Play

Materials: Magpie bridge cutout from Magpie Bridge and Shaped Decorations activity, red and yellow construction paper, string, scissors, adhesive stars, tape, strip of cardboard, glitter

Preparation: Choose two children to act out the mini-play below, following the movements indicated by A and B. Narrate the story as the children act it out.

    Make the Milky Way prop by pressing several stars all over the cardboard strip. Attach two stars, back to back, on the end of each of four short lengths of string. Using tape, attach the other ends of the strings to the cardboard strip so that when the strip is held up the stars on the strings dangle underneath.

    Cut out a red heart and a yellow moon from the paper. Set a low table holding the Milky Way prop, the magpie bridge cutout, the moon, and the heart in front of the players. Have the players stand close together, B to A's right. Have A put an adhesive star on each index finger. B will manipulate the other props on the table. Have the children begin the play by each holding about a teaspoon of glitter in their closed fists, keeping the stars hidden.

Mini-Play: Let us tell a special tale
(A and B hold closed fists to heart and smile.)
That's as bright as a starlit trail.
(A and B throw glitter, then bring hands to sides.)
Altair was the Cowherd Star,
Vega was the Weaver Star.
One day these glittering stars above
Met and fell so much in love.
(A holds up stars, brings them close together,
   B holds up paper heart.)
They decided to go off to play

And forgot their work from day to day.
(A bounces stars around as if running and
    playing.)
"Vega should be weaving!" shouted the
    Heavenly King.
"And Altair's always leaving—he's a playful
    thing!"
So the Heavenly King sent them apart.
This broke the stars' hearts.
(A holds stars apart at arm's length, B returns
    heart to table, frowns.)
But on the seventh day of the seventh moon
    (B holds up moon.)
It was told that Vega could see her friend soon.
(A makes stars bounce for joy, still holding
    them apart.)
But to find Altair on that night
She had to cross the sky and forget her fright.
(B holds Milky Way prop near Vega so that the
    stars dangle underneath.)

Alone and afraid, she had to cross the Milky
    Way,
So the magpies made a bridge that day.
(B puts down Milky Way prop and moon, picks
    up magpie cutout and holds it close to one
    of the stars.)
Up, up, up into the night they flew,
And together their wings made a bridge like
    new!

Vega danced across the magpies' wings,
Humming like a day in spring!
(A dances Vega star over bridge, humming,
    then B puts bridge down.)
She went across to the one she missed
(A holds stars close and presses them
    together.)
And once again, the stars kissed!
(B holds up heart.)

Resources

Birdseye, Tom, *A Song of Stars*, Holiday House, 1990.

Chalmers, Mary, *Easter Parade*, Harper & Row, 1988.

Kraus, Robert, *How Spider Saved Valentine's Day*, Scholastic, 1985.

Kroll, Steven, *Oh, What a Thanksgiving!*, Scholastic, 1988.

Nerlove, Miriam, *Hanukkah*, Albert Whitman, 1989.

Prelutsky, Jack, *It's Halloween*, Scholastic, 1977.

Rockwell, Anne, *Bear Child's Book of Special Days*, Dutton, 1989.

Suid, Anna, *Holiday Crafts*, Monday Morning Books, 1985.

Waters, Kate, and Slovenz-Law, Madeline, *Lion Dancer, Ernie Wan's Chinese New Year*, Scholastic, 1990.